RUSTY WALLACE:
Short Track
to Success

BY BRIAN C. PETERSON

TRADITION BOOKS®
A New Tradition in Children's Publishing™
MAPLE PLAIN, MINNESOTA

Published by **Tradition Books**® and distributed to the
school and library market by **The Child's World**®
P.O. Box 326
Chanhassen, MN 55317-0326
800/599-READ
http://www.childsworld.com

Photo Credits
Cover: Sports Gallery/Al Messerschmidt (2)
AP/Wide World: 13, 14, 18, 19, 20, 24
Corbis: 21
Dick Conway: 5, 6, 8, 10
Sports Gallery: 11, 15, 26 (Al Messerschmidt), 9 (Brian Spurlock), 17, 23, 27, 28 (Joe Robbins)

An Editorial Directions book
Editorial Directions, Inc.: E. Russell Primm, Editorial Director; Katie Marsico and Elizabeth K.
Martin, Assistant Editors; Olivia Nellums, Editorial Assistant; Susan Hindman, Copy Editor;
Susan Ashley, Proofreader; Kevin Cunningham, Fact Checker; Tim Griffin/IndexServ, Indexer;
James Buckley Jr., Photo Researcher and Selector

The Design Lab: Kathy Petelinsek, Art Director and Designer; Kari Thornborough,
Page Production

Library of Congress Cataloging-in-Publication Data
Peterson, Brian C.
  Rusty Wallace : short track to success / by Brian C. Peterson.
      p. cm.—(The world of NASCAR)
Includes index.
Summary: A simple biography of racecar driver Rusty Wallace.
  ISBN 1-59187-032-1 (library bound : alk. paper)
  1. Wallace, Rusty, 1955 or 6– —Juvenile literature. 2. Stock car
drivers—United States—Biography—Juvenile literature. [1. Wallace,
Rusty, 1955 or 6– 2. Automobile racing drivers.] I. Title. II. Series.
GV1032.W35 P48 2003
796.72'092—dc22   2003007688

Printed in the United States of America.

Note: Beginning with the 2004 season, the NASCAR
Winston Cup Series will be called the NASCAR Nextel
Cup Series.

R U S T Y   W A L L A C E

Table of Contents

INTRODUCTION

King of the Road

Many kids dream of sitting behind the wheel of a souped-up stock car. For them, winning the NASCAR Winston Cup Series points championship would be another dream come true. The Winston Cup points title is the greatest achievement a driver can have on the NASCAR circuit.

Russell Wallace Jr., known to everyone as Rusty, began racing full-time in the Winston Cup Series in 1984. Five years later, he was king of the road, capturing the 1989 Winston Cup championship in dramatic fashion.

"In 1989, we made the decision to win," said Wallace in his biography written by Bob Zeller. "I heard a woman tennis player use that term on television, and it hit me right in the head. The 'decision to win' is a whole lot different than saying, 'Oh, we'll do better this year.' The decision to win was expecting more out of your crew than they thought they were going to be putting out. And it was expecting the wives and girlfriends to give up what they didn't want to give up—time with their husbands or boyfriends. It was the team that expected to be together more. It was the decision to work around the clock in the middle of the week to rebuild your **pole-winning** motor,

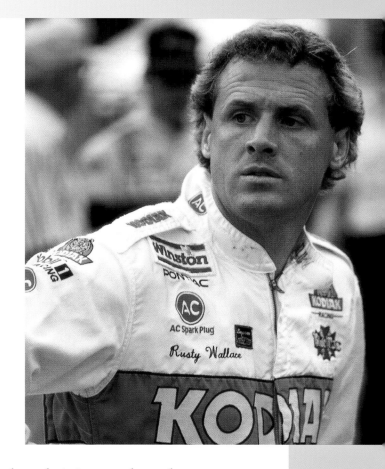

and then taking it to the next track and sitting on the pole again. And this extra effort really paid off."

After finishing second in the Winston Cup points standings in 1988, Wallace's racing team began 1989 with financial problems. Wallace didn't let that stop him, however, and his No. 27 Pontiac came out firing on all cylinders.

Here's Rusty Wallace in 1989, when he became the Winston Cup champion for the first time.

By the end of the season, No. 27 was number one, with a single race remaining. Rusty had to finish 18th or better at Atlanta to clinch the title. He battled some car trouble to squeak into 15th place, good enough for the title.

"No doubt, that 1989 race in Atlanta was my most memorable moment," Wallace said. "It was a squeaker, but we pulled out the championship for that year in that race. There have been a ton of race wins that stick out, but when you look at the big picture, you have to say that winning the '89 championship was the biggest deal yet."

It wasn't the only big deal in this NASCAR veteran's career, however. Here is the story of his long road from the family garage to the top of NASCAR.

Many years of hard work away from the track paid off when this No. 27 car driven by Wallace finished the 1989 season as the best on the track.

C H A P T E R   O N E

Quality Family Time

There are families that play games or go to the movies, and there are families that go fishing, camping, or to Disneyland. Then there is the Wallace family.

Russ and Judy Wallace loved racing, and they spent most weekend evenings with their sons (Rusty, Mike, and Kenny) at racetracks near their home in St. Louis, Missouri. Russ was a fan favorite at area tracks. He is especially successful at Lakehill Speedway, a .3-mile (.48-kilometer) oval in Valley Park, Missouri. Even Judy raced in and won a few events at Lakehill.

"From the time I was ten years old, I was determined to be a race-car driver," Rusty told Zeller. "My dad was a racer. As I worked on his car and watched him race, I knew that's what I wanted to do with my life. [I wanted to] get in a race car and drive it as hard and fast as I could go. My whole family was that way."

In 1972, you had to be 18 to race in Missouri unless your parents gave written consent. When Rusty turned 16, Judy helped him get a court order from a judge so that he could race.

By 1981, Rusty's dream of becoming a pro race driver had come true (though his hair looked a little different back then).

Six days later, Rusty sat behind the wheel of his first race car and won his first race at Lakehill. Rusty even raced against his dad in his first full season at Lakehill. Both Russ and Rusty drove 1969 Chevelles—Russ in the No. 6 car and Rusty in No. 66.

In 1976, the Wallaces took a family trip to Daytona Beach, Florida, to attend **Speedweeks.** Rusty was so smitten with Daytona that he made a vow to return one day and race in NASCAR's Daytona 500.

Rusty's boyhood trip to Daytona's Speedweeks turned into a lifelong love affair with the track, which he returned to here in 2002.

"Racing has been a family deal for us, and it's much more than just the three of us racing," Rusty said. "My dad, Russ, started it all. He was the king of all the tracks around St. Louis for years and won a ton of races and track championships. We owe it all to him because he's responsible for getting us all interested. We owe it to him and my mom for all their support through all these years."

Kenny (green car) and Rusty learned from their dad Russ how to bang their way ahead in stock car racing.

THE BROTHERS WALLACE

The racing bug bit everyone in the Wallace family. Rusty has become the most well known of the three Wallace brothers, but that doesn't mean that Kenny and Mike haven't had their share of success in NASCAR.

In 2002, Kenny finished seventh in the NASCAR **Busch Series** points standings. He has nine career Busch Series victories and was named the Busch Series rookie of the year in 1989. In 1991, Kenny finished second to Bobby Labonte in the Busch Series points standings.

Mike has been one of NASCAR's most versatile drivers, competing on all three levels: **Craftsman Truck Series,** Busch Series, and Winston Cup. At the 2001 Daytona 500, Mike had a career-best sixth-place finish, while Rusty finished third. Mike also won the inaugural truck series race at Daytona in 2000.

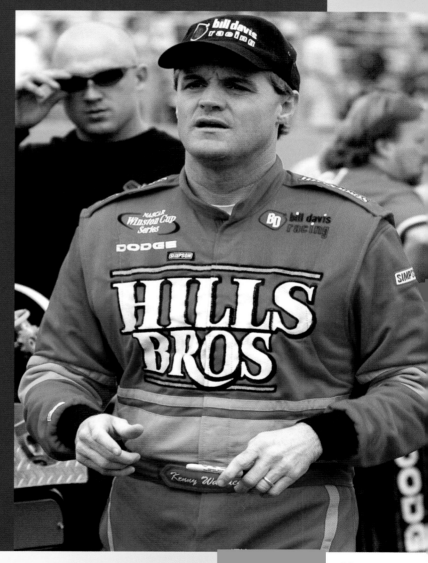

Kenny Wallace has enjoyed a lot of success in the Busch Series, one step below the Winston Cup level.

CHAPTER TWO

Grease Monkey

If you don't have sponsors in racing, you often have to do everything yourself if you want to succeed. That's exactly what Rusty Wallace did.

Wallace and his brothers made extra money as kids delivering newspapers or working for their dad at his vacuum repair shop. They spent the rest of their time tinkering with cars. In fact, your nose could tell you if the Wallace boys were around. They usually showed up at school smelling like oil and gas because of all the time they spent with cars.

By age 15, Rusty was a proficient car **fabricator** and mechanic, and a regular member of his dad's pit crew. He had to attend summer school to graduate from high school because he had spent so much time working on cars.

"I knew a lot about race cars before I ever drove one," Rusty told Zeller. "I was helping my dad prepare his car all the time."

After graduating from high school, Wallace took a job in a machine shop doing valve jobs and rebuilding motors. In November 1975, he formed the Poor Boy **Chassis** Company with Don Miller, who worked for famous race team owner Roger Penske. Wallace built and raced his own cars for the first 12 years of his racing career. His love for working on cars still burns strong today. Wallace will get under his car to check things and isn't afraid to get his hands dirty.

A long way from his roots, but still in the garage: Here, Rusty meets with 2003 crew chief Bill Wilburn about how his car is running.

In 1998, he and Penske debuted the new Ford Taurus
car, which they had helped create with the Ford Motor
Company. During 2002 and 2003, Wallace has written
"Rusty's Rundown," a weekly in-depth analysis of each
week's Winston Cup race on NASCAR.com.

Rusty's new Ford Taurus (No. 2 car) trails two legends,
Dale Earnhardt Sr. (No. 3) and Jeff Gordon (No. 24) in
this 1998 race.

LEGAL RACER

Greg Wallace, Rusty's oldest son, didn't have to get a court order to be able to begin racing. Greg might be needing court orders in the future, however. He graduated from Hampden-Sydney College (in Virginia) in 2000 and planned on attending law school.

Racing, however, has interrupted Greg's desire to become a lawyer. Greg raced in the Late Model Division and also served as a **spotter** for Rusty during the 2002 NASCAR season.

"When he comes across the radio, it's like crystal clear," Rusty said. "I really make out every word he says. He's kind of hyper like me, so it's, 'Clear high! High! Low! Low! Low!' It's not like, 'Oh . . . they're . . . looking . . . inside.'"

"I've been around race cars my entire life," Greg said. "I can't tell you how many of these races I've been to, and at every race, I listen to the headsets. You pick up on the lingo and stuff like that."

Drivers and crew chiefs rely on spotters like these, who stand on tall towers around the track. They communicate via radio with the crew and drivers.

Short Track to Success

Survival and crafty driving are the keys to winning on NASCAR's shorter tracks. Those include the tracks at Bristol in Tennessee and at Richmond and Martinsville in Virginia. Cars never finish a **short-track** race without countless dents and scrapes.

Almost all NASCAR Winston Cup Series drivers cut their racing teeth on short tracks, and Rusty Wallace was no different. From 1974 to 1978, he won more than 200 short-track races at levels below Winston Cup. During the late '70s and early '80s, Wallace drove with his own car and team across America, racing on short tracks from Florida to California.

Wallace and his mostly volunteer team, nicknamed "The Evil Gang," transported their car in an old bread truck they called "The Hilton." The Evil Gang, whose members included

Rusty and his brothers, did not have a lot of money. The Hilton was their home on the road, and winning races was their reward.

"I remember running on all the bullrings across the country," Rusty says. "We towed our short-track car behind the Hilton. [My friend] Paul Andrews was my crew chief back then, and my brother Kenny worked with us a bunch. When you look back at the roots we came from, it definitely is amazing what I have been able to accomplish in my career."

Rusty Wallace is one of the most successful short-track drivers ever. Here, he rides the tight curves of the Bristol Speedway in Tennessee.

In 1983, Wallace decided to focus his attention on the American Speed Association (ASA) short-track stock-car series. The ASA was the premier short-track series in the Midwest. Wallace concluded his short-track career by winning the ASA championship that year.

Wallace switched to the NASCAR Winston Cup Series full-time in 1984. Not surprisingly, he won his first two Winston Cup races on the short tracks at Bristol and Martinsville in 1986. Wallace has won 24 short-track Winston Cup races in all. At those tracks, he has finished in the top five of those races 47 percent of the time and in the top 10 nearly 70 percent of the time.

The cars of both Rusty Wallace (No. 2) and Bobby Labonte (No. 18) show the effects of racing in tight packs at the Martinsville, Virginia, track.

From 1992 to 2001, Wallace had an amazing 23 consecutive top-10 finishes on short tracks. In 1993, he put together one of the greatest seasons in NASCAR history on the short tracks, winning five of eight short-track races and finishing second in the other three.

"When the history book on the modern era of NASCAR racing is written, I don't want to be remembered as just a good short-track driver," Wallace said. "I want to be remembered

Rusty celebrates yet another short-track win, this one at Dover Downs in Delaware in 1993.

as a top competitor at all of the tracks. Sure, we've been really competitive on the small tracks, but we've won at Charlotte, Michigan, Pocono, and [other big] tracks, too. I want to be remembered as a well-rounded competitor."

A big smile for a big-track win: Rusty shares a victory hug with crew chief Barry Dodson after winning the 1988 600-mile (965-km) race at Charlotte Motor Speedway in North Carolina.

HIGH FLYER

Even Rusty Wallace's favorite hobby provides some high-speed thrills. Wallace began flying in 1982 and got his pilot's license in 1984. Today, Wallace owns Diamond Aviation, which has a Lear jet, another plane, and a long-range helicopter. For a man who spends his workdays speeding on the ground in heavy traffic, a trip to the skies is a welcome relief.

"The first time I ever flew in a small airplane, there wasn't a cloud in the sky," Wallace said. "It was beautiful. Of course, it's great for avoiding all of this race traffic!"

Talk about high speed! Rusty not only drives fast cars, he pilots fast Lear jets like these.

CHAPTER FOUR

Trips down Victory Lane

———

R usty Wallace is one of the winningest drivers in NASCAR history. His 54 Winston Cup series victories currently place him eighth on the circuit's all-time list.

Wallace took the checkered flag in at least one race for 16 consecutive seasons (1986–2001). That mark ties Ricky Rudd for the longest modern-day streak in NASCAR. Richard Petty set NASCAR's all-time record with at least one victory in 18 consecutive seasons from 1960 to 1977.

Wallace's streak ended in 2002, but that didn't mean he was less of a force. In 2002, he placed seventh in the Winston Cup points standings. Along the way, he had 7 top-five finishes, 17 top-tens, and earned more than $4 million. He finished second in four races, including events at Daytona, Indianapolis, Bristol, and Phoenix.

In 2002, Rusty and his crew moved (a lot faster than in this picture!) to 17 top-ten finishes, including four second-place spots.

It has been a wonderful racing career for Wallace, who has come a long way since his rookie season of 1984. That year, he earned a meager $40,000 salary and was named NASCAR's rookie of the year. He did so despite blowing up numerous engines and crashing often.

Here's a great "comin' at ya" view of Rusty Wallace leading a big pack of NASCAR cars out of a turn at the big Michigan Speedway.

Today, with more than $33 million in career earnings, Wallace has won around 10 percent of his career Winston Cup starts. He captured 10 victories in 1993, including three consecutive wins at Bristol, North Wilkesboro, and Martinsville. In 1994, he again won three races in a row (Dover, Pocono, and Michigan) and totaled eight victories.

A model of consistency, Wallace has placed among the top-10 points leaders in 16 of his 19 seasons. In more than half of his 598 career races, he has finished in the top 10.

Wallace has been brilliant on short tracks, road courses, and **superspeedways.** He has survived violent crashes, overcome financial problems, and defeated opponents by the narrowest of margins. And through it all, Wallace was a man on a mission, crafting a legendary career in the sport he truly loved.

"If I learned one thing along the way it's the power of persistence," Wallace wrote on NASCAR.com. "If you absolutely positively commit to do something, then you're

probably going to do it well. I've succeeded at the highest
levels of my sport because I was bound and determined to
do it. But we also never lost sight of having a little fun along
the way."

Since he was a little kid, this is the place that Rusty
Wallace has wanted to be: In the driver's seat of a
stock car, ready for racin'!

RUSTY THE ENDORSER

Rusty Wallace's energetic personality has attracted a strong following of fans throughout his racing career. Because of his widespread popularity, he has become one of NASCAR's highest-profile spokespersons.

In 2001, he teamed with Carnival Cruise Lines and sailed with more than 2,000 members of the Rusty Wallace Fan Club throughout the Caribbean. (Wallace actually got to steer the ship.)

He has had numerous corporate sponsors in his career. One of the most unique came in 2002 when he partnered with Planters Nuts. Mr. Peanut, the Planters' icon, was featured on Wallace's uniform.

Wallace also has one of the coolest Web sites (www.rustywallace.com) on the Internet, and his wife, Patti, oversees his fan club. In 2003, he was the spokesperson for NASCAR in Car on Demand, the pay-per-view digital cable television service offered by NASCAR.

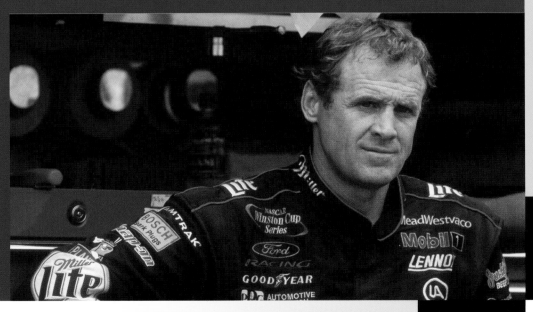

See if you can find Mr. Peanut among Rusty's many sponsor logos. Hint: Mr. Peanut has something up his sleeve.

28   **Just moments before the race starts, Rusty thinks about the action ahead . . . and about capturing the checkered flag!**

RUSTY WALLACE'S LIFE

1956   Born on August 14 in Fenton, Missouri

1973   On April 12, officially begins his racing career at Lakehill
Speedway in Valley Park, Missouri; wins first race

Named Central Auto Racing Association rookie of the year

1979   Joins the U.S. Auto Club (USAC) stock-car circuit and wins rookie-
of-the-year honors; wins five USAC races and finishes second in
overall points standings

1981   Marries Patti Hall

1983   Wins American Speed Association (ASA) short-track stock-car
series points championship

1984   Joins NASCAR Winston Cup Series full-time and wins rookie-of-
the-year honors

1986   Wins first Winston Cup race, the Valleydale 500 at Bristol,
Tennessee

1987   Wins first NASCAR pole at Michigan International Speedway

1988   Finishes second in Winston Cup points standings

1989   Wins Winston Cup Series points championship

1993   Finishes second in Winston Cup points standings, winning
10 races

1994   Wins eight races

1998   Inducted into the Missouri Sports Hall of Fame

2001   Wins at least one race in sixteen consecutive seasons, tying Ricky
Rudd for a NASCAR modern-day record

GLOSSARY

Busch Series—one level below Winston Cup; the races are shorter and the cars are slightly smaller

chassis—the steel frame of a car

Craftsman Truck Series—a NASCAR racing event in which drivers race closed-bed pickup trucks at the same tracks as Winston Cup and Busch Series events

fabricator—team member who puts sheet metal on the car's frame and molds it to the shape of the car, creating the body or outside shell of the car

pole-winner—the racer who has the fastest qualifying time and can then start a race on the inside of the front line, or the "pole position"

short track—racetracks shorter than 1 mile (1.6 km) in length

Speedweeks—a series of racing events—held during the two weeks leading up to the Daytona 500—that helps kick off each NASCAR season at Daytona International Speedway

spotter—a team member who watches a race from on top of the grandstands or press box and acts as the driver's second set of eyes, telling the driver where to go on the racetrack to avoid an accident or when to pass another car

superspeedway—an oval racetrack of 2.5 miles (4 km) or more in length

FOR MORE INFORMATION ABOUT RUSTY WALLACE

Books

Martin, Mark. *NASCAR for Dummies.* New York: Wiley Publishing, Inc., 2000.

Mello, Tara Baukus. *Rusty Wallace.* Philadelphia: Chelsea House Publishers, 1998.

Zeller, Bob, with foreword by Rusty Wallace. *Rusty Wallace: The Decision to Win.* Phoenix: David Bull Publishing, 1999.

Web Sites

ESPN's NASCAR section
http://rpm.espn.go.com/rpm/index
For complete coverage of all NASCAR events from one of the nation's leading sports information providers

The Official Web Site of NASCAR
http://www.nascar.com
For an overview of each season of NASCAR, as well as the history of the sport, statistics, and a dictionary of racing terms

The Official Web Site of Rusty Wallace
http://www.rustywallace.com
For loads of information on Rusty Wallace on his official site, including a way to e-mail questions to him and his team

Sporting News
http://www.sportingnews.com/nascar/
For another great source of NASCAR information

INDEX

ABOUT THE AUTHOR

Brian C. Peterson has been a professional sportswriter for more than a decade. He has written two books, *Terrell Davis* and *NFL Rules!* and his articles have appeared in publications such as the *New York Times, Boston Globe, NFL Insider,* and *NFL GameDay.* Peterson resides with his wife and two young children in Torrance, California.